FAST ATTACK CRAFT

FAST ATTACK CRAFT

Anthony J. Watts

1. During the 1970s a number of smaller navies began to acquire modern FACs. Among them were the navies of South America. Seen here is the Venezuela Navy's Vosper Thornycroft 121ft *Constitución*. This class, commissioned in 1974–5, comprised six units, three of which were armed with Italian OTOMAT surface-surface missiles. *Constitución* was a gun-armed boat carrying a single 76mm forward and a single 40mm aft. Machinery comprised two MTU diesels which gave the boats a maximum speed of 31 knots. (Maritime World Photo Library)

ARMS AND
ARMOUR

Arms and Armour Press
A Cassell Imprint
Villiers House, 41-47 Strand,
London WC2N 5JE.

Distributed in the USA by Sterling Publishing Co. Inc., 387 Park Avenue South, New York, NY 10016-8810.

Distributed in Australia by Capricorn Link (Australia) Pty. Ltd, P.O. Box 665, Lane Cove, New South Wales 2066.

Designed and edited by DAG Publications Ltd. Designed by David Gibbons; edited by Michael Boxall; layout by Anthony A. Evans; typeset by Typesetters (Birmingham) Limited, Warley, West Midlands; camerawork by M&E Reproductions, North Fambridge, Essex; printed and bound in Great Britain by The Bath Press, Avon.

British Library Cataloguing in Publication Data
Watts, Anthony J. (Anthony John), *1942–*
Fast attack craft.
I. Title
623.825
ISBN 1-85409-081-X

INTRODUCTION

At the end of the Second World War the large fleets of fast MTBs (Motor Torpedo Boats), MGBs (Motor Gunboats), PT Boats, MAS boats and E-boats which formed the bulk of coastal forces of the Royal Navy, US Navy, Italian Navy and the Reichsmarine, and which were designed for use in narrow waters, were quickly hulked and scrapped. With only the Royal and US Navies retaining a token force of such craft, it seemed as if the days (actually nights!) of hectic action by swarms of small high-speed boats tearing about the North Sea, Aegean or Pacific torpedoing unsuspecting targets before retiring at high speed, all guns blazing, were firmly in the past. The deployment and usefulness of these boats was based on the element of surprise, but with the advent of much more sophisticated radars, and lacking the ability to engage from ranges beyond those commanded by other warships, it appeared as if there was no longer a role for this type of vessel. As a result, development of these craft came to a virtual standstill after the end of the Second World War. Some work continued, albeit at a very slow pace, the British re-engining an old gunboat with two Rolls-Royce RM.60 gas turbines to achieve the required power for the higher speeds then considered necessary.

2. The years immediately following the Second World War saw a vast rundown in the enormous fleets of MTBs and MGBs that had captured the headlines during the war. Many boats were sold off to smaller naval powers. Such construction of small fast craft as was still undertaken was largely based on wartime concepts of high-speed motor torpedo-boats or motor gunboats (MTBs or MGBs). Typical of these was the Norwegian *Laks*, an ex-US PT boat completed in 1945 and handed over to the Norwegian Navy in 1951 under the Mutual Defence Aid Program (MDAP). (Michael Lennon via Maritime World Photo Library)

During the 1950s and 1960s the German yard Lürssen Werft led the field in high-speed attack craft design with the production of torpedo/gunboats for the Swedish and newly formed German Navies. The company then developed the classical 45m and 57m export designs on which many others have since been based, including the successful French 'Combattante' and Israeli 'Saar' classes. Development work on newer and more powerful machinery continued, but, apart from a brief foray into gas turbine propulsion systems, which did not achieve the hoped-for popularity, remained in the sphere of high-speed diesel engines.

During the 1960s developments took place which were to transform the capability of small boats, giving them a new lease of life and enabling designers to develop vessels with much greater radius of action than the old petrol-engined craft, and with a much more powerful armament, and hence destructive capability. The development of lightweight, unmanned medium calibre (57mm and 76mm) guns with compact fire control and servo systems (which themselves had been developed following the emergence of the transistor and micro-electronics which replaced the old thermionic valves in radio, radar and electronic surveillance systems) designed to keep weapons well on target, revolutionized the science of small ship gunnery. At the same time the advent of surface-to-surface missiles carried in a fairly small container enabled the fast attack craft (FAC), as these small craft came to be known, to engage much larger targets on advantageous terms and at far longer ranges than had been associated with the fast torpedo-boats of the past. Deck-mounted lightweight guided torpedoes and, in the last decade, effective detection sonars have continued to augment the armoury, although lack of deck space and the instability of the smaller ship platform in a seaway generally precludes helicopter operations. Helicopters are, of course, highly effective in ASW, targeting, surveillance and transport roles, and consideration of their inclusion in weapon systems has prompted some navies to choose larger FACs capable of deploying them.

The modern FAC is vastly different from the old torpedo-boats of the Second World War. Today's FAC is much larger, with greatly improved seakeeping qualities and much more powerful armament. The majority of modern, conventional, semi-displacement FACs, capable of packing a powerful punch, as distinct from offshore patrol vessels or hybrid coast guard craft, tend to be built in sizes ranging from 35 to 57 metres in length, but stretches to just over 60 metres when helicopter operations are stated as a requirement. There have also been a few notable missile hydrofoils developed, but hovercraft have never really become established as attack craft.

To achieve the high speeds required in the old torpedo-boats meant that most of the interior space aboard was taken up by the engines. Fuel consumption was high and bunker space limited which left little room for accommodation, and so the craft were used essentially for short-range operations so that they could return to base at night, or lie up in some sheltered spot overnight to allow their crews to rest. The development of marine gas turbines offering great power and speed in lightweight installations appeared to be the obvious answer for new generations of FACs in the 1950s, but more economical turbo-charged diesels, able to offer good sprint and long-range cruise speeds, returned to favour and predominate today, coupled with the use of either fixed pitch or controllable pitch propellers, though waterjets are beginning to make an impact.

Most of the interior of the modern FAC is still taken up by powerful machinery, and although much-improved accommodation and air conditioning for operations in Arctic or tropical waters is now provided, they are not really designed for long-range ocean operations. But FACs have undertaken very long sea voyages, although this is not their normal mode of operation. Admittedly FACs are no longer tasked with patrols of just a few hours' duration, but endurance is still measured in days rather than weeks, and in rough weather the crew of even a modern FAC will quickly become tired from the buffeting and the noise and smells associated with what are still fairly cramped quarters.

Today many of the world's navies operate heavily armed FACs; they may form the major strike force of smaller navies whose prime task is coastal defence. While no substitute for ocean-going ships requiring long endurance and prolonged heavy weather capability, FACs ranging in displacement up to 500 tons or more offer fast, manoeuvrable and, in many respects, less vulnerable platforms, than corvettes or frigates. Coupled with this is their comparative economy of construction which may allow larger, and therefore more effective, fleets to be built.

FACs are favoured principally by the countries of the Soviet bloc, the Far East, Mediterranean and Baltic, together with Third World navies. The Third World preference for the FAC is easily understood, from an economic viewpoint – larger ships, certainly in any numbers, will be unaffordable. FACs may also double as coastguard, anti-piracy, anti-smuggling and fishery protection craft – duties which are far more realistic than attempting to establish an ocean-going naval presence. Maritime geography plays an important part in the choice of such craft. In narrow, sheltered, island-strewn and shallow waters, FACs designed for speed, manoeuvrability and stealth have a positive advantage over larger warships. Where the security and defence of long and broken coastlines is a priority, strategically stationed FACs can also provide the ideal answer.

3. Although having deployed huge numbers of MTBs and MGBs during the war, the Royal Navy maintained only a token force of these post-war. A number of Dark and Gay-class small MTBs/MGBs were built along more or less traditional lines. However, the Royal Navy did undertake experimental design work on small fast craft and following the construction of two experimental Bold-class MTBs built of light alloy and powered by two gas turbines and two diesels, proceeded to construct two Brave-class MTB/MGB-type boats. Like the Bold class, these were built by Vosper Ltd at Portsmouth with welded aluminium hull framing covered with double-skinned mahogany planking and sheathed with glass fibre below the waterline. The two boats were powered by PROTEUS gas turbines, the first of this type of craft to be powered solely by gas turbines. On speed trials they reached speeds in excess of 50 knots. It was originally intended that they would carry a specially designed 3.3in stabilized gun mount, but this was later removed and the boats were armed with two 40mm guns and/or torpedo tubes. (Maritime World Photo Library)

4. At the beginning of the 1960s the Soviet Union, which had always possessed a large fleet of small craft, developed a small missile, the SS-N-2, commonly referred to as the STYX, which could be mounted on the hull of a motor torpedo-boat. Known as the Komar-class guided missile boats, they were built in large numbers and a great many were exported. The advent of these missile-armed craft was to revolutionize small, fast boat design and development for the next 20–30 years, leading to a whole new generation of missile attack craft being built in large numbers throughout the world. As the missiles and craft developed, virtually every navy in the world managed to acquire some form of missile-armed attack craft, which then posed a major threat to most types of surface warship, except the largest and most powerfully armed. The potency of this threat was eventually revealed on 21 October 1967 when an Egyptian missile-armed Komar craft sank the Israeli destroyer *Eilath* during the Six Day War. The Komar missile boats seen here were photographed at Algiers in 1968. (Maritime World Photo Library)

5

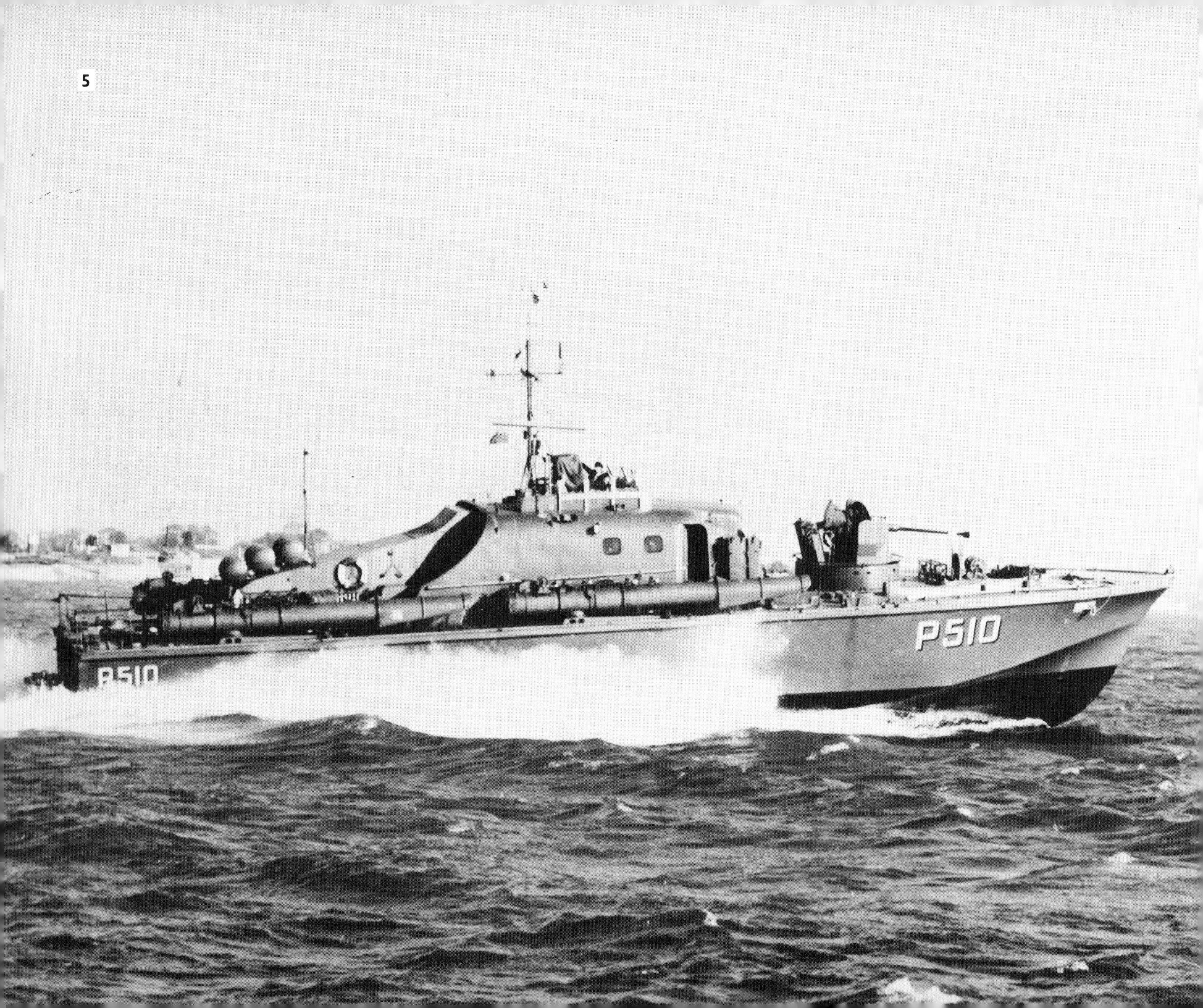

5. Although the Royal Navy showed little real interest in developing the fast attack craft concept, the designs developed in the UK were exported. A development of the Brave design, combining features of another British fast attack craft, the *Ferocity*, resulted in the six boats of the Danish Soloven-class, of which *Soloven* is seen here. Completed between 1964 and 1967, they were powered by three PROTEUS gas turbines and armed with two 40mm and four 21in torpedo tubes. (Maritime World Photo Library)

6. At the beginning of the 1960s the Russians began building a larger missile-armed fast attack craft, the Osa-class. Whiel the Komar-class boats carried only two missile-launchers, these larger boats were fitted with two pairs of launchers abreast the small superstructure. The SS-N-2 STYX had a range of 15–18 miles. Gun armament comprised two twin 30mm, one mount forward and one aft. The Osa class was widely exported. (Maritime World Photo Library)

7. A Soviet Osa I-class FAC firing a STYX missile. While small enough to fit on a FAC, the missile is, nevertheless, still a fairly large weapon. The missile first began to enter service in 1959–60 and is still operational with many FACs around the world. In addition to being used during the Six Day War, the STYX missile was also fired in anger during the Indo–Pakistani War in December 1971. It is used in a coastal defence role by Syrian and Yugoslav forces, and, until the break up of the Warsaw Pact, was used by the East German forces. The missile seen here is the SS-N-2a with fixed wings. A boost motor accelerates the missile from the moment of launch to reach cruise speed of Mach 0.9, after which an internal motor sustains the missile at cruise speed. In the photograph the internal motor has just ignited and the boost motor is nearing the end of its endurance (seen under the body of the missile), after which it will be jettisoned. The 5.8m-long missile carries a charge of 450kg of HE to a range of about 40 kilometres. (Maritime World Photo Library)

6

7

8. Soviet sailors race to man a flotilla of Osa I FACs during an exercise. (Maritime World Photo Library)

9. A flotilla of Osa I FACs returns to base after an exercise. (Maritime World Photo Library)

10. An Osa I-class FAC. (Maritime World Photo Library)

11 and 12. From the mid 1960s the Soviets embarked on a large construction programme of FACs armed with both missiles and torpedoes. The torpedo-armed Shershen class, like the Komars and Osas, was also widely exported. Seen here is No. 832, *Erich Kuttner*, of the former East German Navy. The boats are armed with four 21in torpedo tubes designed to fire the Soviet Type 53 dual-purpose, active/passive homing torpedo which has a range of about 20 kilometres. The weapon carries a high-explosive warhead of about 400kg at speeds up to 45 knots. In addition to the torpedo tubes there are two twin 30mm gun mounts. Powered by three diesels, the Shershen class has a maximum speed in the region of 45 knots. (Maritime World Photo Library)

13. Construction of Shershen-class FACs ended in about 1974. They are now considered obsolete and many are being scrapped. Seen here is the East German Navy's *Ernst Grube* (No. 853) being scrapped in June 1990. (Maritime World Photo Library)

14. An Egyptian Shershen-class FAC is seen here with two BM21 multiple rocket-launchers mounted in place of the torpedo tubes, and an SA-N-5 GRAIL surface-to-air missile-launcher. The FAC was photographed in Port Said in May 1974. (Maritime World Photo Library)

15. The Soviets continued to develop their FAC designs, and with the introduction of the SS-N-2B STYX anti-ship missile, which incorporated folding wings, the Osa II class was designed. These units differed from the Osa I in having a new, smaller missile-launcher mounted in pairs just abaft the bridge. (Maritime World Photo Library)

16 and 17. Towards the end of the 1960s the Royal Navy ordered another three fast patrol boats whose design was developed from that of the earlier Brave class. Powered by two Rolls-Royce PROTEUS gas turbines, these three Vosper Thornycroft boats (*Cutlass, Sabre* and *Scimitar*), of glued laminated wood construction, remained unarmed, although having the capability to mount a gun/missile armament if required, and also a third gas turbine. They were used extensively as training boats, principally in exercises designed to simulate attack by fast missile craft against RN frigates and destroyers. They were sold in the early 1980s. (Maritime World Photo Library)

18. In 1968–9 Vosper Thornycroft built the fast patrol boat *Tenacity* as a private venture. With steel hull and aluminium superstructure, *Tenacity* was designed to capture what was becoming a burgeoning market in fast attack craft. During a short demonstration period the vessel was fitted out with a number of mock missile configurations and fire control systems in an effort to interest overseas customers. *Tenacity* was eventually purchased by the Royal Navy in January 1972 for evaluation purposes. Failing to find a fast attack mission profile in line with RN commitments, she was refitted with a light armament and used on fishery protection duties, being finally set aside for disposal at the beginning of the 1980s. (Maritime World Photo Library)

19. Early in the 1960s China began a large programme of fast attack boat construction, the most numerous being the 'Shanghai' type, built in five versions, of which more than 320 are now in service with the Chinese Navy. In addition, numerous units are operational with Third World Navies. The boat seen here is P 106 of the Zairean Navy. All units are gun armed with two twin 37mm and four 25mm. The design is now considered obsolete; many units are no longer operational and many are being scrapped. (G. Gilbert via Maritime World Photo Library)

20

20 and 21. In Russia fast attack craft types continued to multiply. Another large class of fast attack craft, the Stenkas, of which more than 122 have been completed, was based on the design of the Osas. Construction began in 1967; the boats are armed with four 400mm torpedo tubes and two twin 30mm guns. They are powered by three diesels which give them a top speed of 36 knots. (Maritime World Photo Library)

'22

22. From 1957 until the late 1960s the Soviets also built 150 boats of the SO.1 class. Although not strictly fast attack craft, these steel-hulled units were primarily designed for anti-submarine warfare, being armed with four 5-barrelled A/S rocket-projectors and in some units two A/S torpedo tubes. The photograph shows the A/S rocket-launchers mounted forward on an SO.1 boat. Behind them can be seen a twin 25mm mounting. The boats were powered by three diesels and had a maximum speed of 28 knots. (Maritime World Photo Library)

23 and 24. Hydrofoils were also built in large numbers by the Soviets. From 1972 to 1978 a total of 34 Turya class were built for the Soviet Navy, and construction for export continued thereafter. These large (250-ton) hydrofoils had a length of 40 metres and were propelled by three powerful diesels which gave them a speed of 40 knots foilborne. Armament comprised two 57mm in a twin mount aft, and two 25mm forward. They also carried four 533mm torpedo tubes together with the usual fire control radar, etc. Soviet Navy units also carry a variable-depth sonar. Like the Stenkas, the design was basically that of an Osa with hydrofoils added. (Maritime World Photo Library)

23

24

25. The Soviets continued to export large numbers of Osas, the unit seen here being an Osa I of the Egyptian Navy. (Maritime World Photo Library)

26. Shortly after Venezuela acquired her FACs, Ecuador also acquired a class of three German Lürssen-built craft. Commissioned in 1976–7 these larger units (147ft as opposed to 121ft) were armed with four French EXOCET surface-surface missiles aft and a single 76mm gun forward and twin 35mm aft. The boats were powered by four MTU diesels which gave them a maximum speed of 40 knots. (Maritime World Photo Library)

27. During the 1960s the Norwegian Navy commissioned a large class of twenty Storm-class gun-armed fast attack craft. Originally they were built as purely gun-armed boats, with a large 76mm gun forward and a 40mm aft, but with the introduction of the PENGUIN anti-ship missile, boats in the class were gradually armed with six missile-launchers from 1970 onwards. (Maritime World Photo Library)

28. The Storm class were followed by the six vessels of the Snogg class, with steel hulls similar to the Storm boats. The Snogg-class (*Snar* is seen here at speed in a Norwegian fiord) entered service from 1970 onwards, armed with four PENGUIN missile-launchers, four 21in torpedo tubes and a single 40mm gun forward.

29. The Norwegian fast attack craft *Terne* is one of fourteen Hauk-class

27

boats completed from 1977 to 1980. They carry a mix of armament including both torpedo tubes and missiles. The two 21in torpedo tubes can be clearly seen mounted on each side of the hull just forward of the bridge.

Aft can be seen two missile-launchers for PENGUIN anti-ship missiles. In some boats an extra two/four launchers are mounted abreast the after gun mount. A single 40mm gun is carried in a mount in front of the bridge, and a single 20mm gun aft. The weapon control system is a Norwegian-developed MSI-80S system. Powered by two German MTU diesels, the boats reach a maximum speed of 34 knots. Overall length is 36.5 metres and beam 6.2 metres. The photograph shows *Terne* firing a PENGUIN missile. (Maritime World Photo Library)

30. One of the early post-war Federal German Navy fast attack craft classes was the Jaguar class. A total of 40 of these were built from 1957 to 1964, of which *Wiesel* is seen here. These boats were armed with two 40mm guns in single mounts and carried four 21in torpedo tubes. Ten of them, including *Wiesel*, were subsequently modified with new fire control systems and torpedo arma-

ment reduced to two tubes. As such they were known as the Zobel class. (Maritime World Photo Library)

31. During the 1970s the Federal German Navy commissioned a class of twenty Type 148 fast attack craft designed by the famous French yard of CMN at Cherbourg and based on their famous Combattante design which sold in large numbers to many

navies around the world during the 1970s and early 1980s. The steel hulls of eight of this class, although built by the German Lürssen yard, were fitted out by CMN. Armament comprised four of the ubiquitous EXOCET anti-ship missiles which have achieved spectacular successes in various conflicts since they were introduced into service. In addition to the missiles (the boat seen here

S41 – P6141, carried the EXOCET launching rails, but the missiles are not mounted), a single 76mm gun is mounted forward and a single 40mm right aft. Power is provided by four MTU diesels, which give the boats a maximum speed of 33.5 knots. French Thomson CSF fire control systems and radars are mounted. (Maritime World Photo Library)

32

32. In the early 1970s the Italian Navy embarked on a missile hydrofoil programme. The first unit, *Sparviero*, was completed in July 1974, but the remaining six boats were not commissioned until the early 1980s. These boats differ from most other missile craft in that there is no sleeping accommodation, the tactical concept being that the boats operate near to the coast within day range of their bases. Powered by a single Rolls-Royce PROTEUS gas turbine and General Motors diesel in a combined diesel or gas turbine combination, maximum speed is 40 knots. These boats are armed with two of the powerful OTOMAT anti-ship missiles with a range greater than the EXOCET. The boats also mount a 76mm forward. On a length of only 24.6 metres and beam of 7 metres, these highly manoeuvrable boats are extremely powerful. Italy has now sold the design licence to Japan who will build twelve of them for the Japanese Maritime Self-Defence Force. (Maritime World Photo Library)

33. In such a small craft as the Italian hydrofoil *Sparviero*, space is at a premium. The photograph shows the bridge accommodation with, on the left, the seat for the helmsman, who also controls the engines, and to the right the navigating position with the radar. Despite the cramped space, all-round view is particularly good in these craft. (Maritime World Photo Library)

34. The machinery control console aboard the *Sparviero*-class hydrofoil. (Maritime World Photo Library)

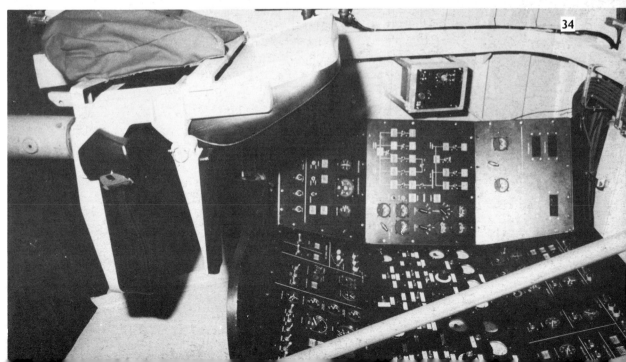

35. In the early 1970s the United States embarked on a programme of hydrofoil construction with the intention of deploying a fleet of high-speed attack craft. PHM 1, the USS *Pegasus*, made her first foilborne trip on 25 February 1975. However, the programme was cancelled two years later, leaving only *Pegasus* which was to be used as a high-speed test vehicle. Following heavy Congressional pressure, the programme was reinstated in August 1977 and funds were made available to complete the programme of six boats. The design of these craft was developed using the experience of the Italian Navy, which had already undertaken construction of the *Sparviero*-class boats, and the Federal German Navy. The intention was to develop a small, high-speed attack craft that would, with minor modifications, be able to meet the small, high-speed craft requirement of all the NATO navies. In the event, only the Americans built the hydrofoils. The 40.5m craft are powered by a General Electric LM 2500 gas turbine developing 18,000shp to power Aerojet waterjet units. For hullborne propulsion two MTU diesels are fitted. Maximum speed foilborne is 48 knots. Armament comprises eight HARPOON surface-surface missiles and a 76mm gun forward. The boats are fitted with comprehensive electronic warfare systems including intercept sensors, jammers and chaff, and infra-red decoys. Weapons are controlled from a fully integrated fire control system, and comprehensive communications are carried. (Maritime World Photo Library)

36. This aerial view of PHM 4, the USS *Taurus*, shows clearly the deck layout of the hydrofoil. Recessed into the hull aft can be seen the powerful hydraulic arms which raise and lower the foils. Only two HAR-POON anti-ship missile-launchers are mounted. (Maritime World Photo Library)

A. The *Istiqlal* was one of two German Lürssen-designed and built FACs delivered to Kuwait in 1982 and 1983. These large, powerful craft were designed to operate as flotilla leaders for the six smaller Kuwaiti TNC 45-type FACs. Their armament and electronics were identical with those of the smaller TNC 45s, but they had extended communications facilities, improved accommodation and extended superstructure and rails aft for laying mines. (Maritime World Photo Library)

B. The Kuwaiti TNC 45 craft *Jalboot* (later renamed *Al Sanbouk*) is seen here on contractor's trials. Built and designed by Lürssen in Germany, the six 45m-long FACs of this type were ordered in 1980 and delivered in 1982, when the crews underwent an extensive period of training before the craft were finally accepted in 1984. They are powerfully armed, carrying four French EXOCET anti-ship missiles, Italian 76mm and twin 40mm guns, backed up by a comprehensive electronic outfit comprising a British navigation radar, a Swedish 9LV 200 search radar, 9LV 200 fire control system, British CUTLASS electronic warfare system, French Chaff dispenser and French optical sight. They are powered by four German diesels giving a maximum speed in the region of 40 knots. A number of the class was captured by Iraq in 1990 and subsequently destroyed. So far actual losses have not been confirmed. (Maritime World Photo Library)

C. In 1987 the Italian shipyard Fincantieri built the FAC *Saettia* as a speculative venture, the craft being used to demonstrate new concepts in ship design for FACs. One of the major features of the design was the very much reduced silhouette with carefully angled corners designed to minimize the radar signature of the vessel. This distinctive form of silhouette has since been imitated in other FAC designs. (Maritime World Photo Library)

D. The Peruvian FAC *Herrera* was built by SFCN in France and commissioned in 1981. She is one of a class of six PR-72P-type craft whose design dates back to the early 1970s. Like many FACs around the world, these craft are armed with the ubiquitous French EXOCET anti-ship missile and Italian 76mm and twin 40mm guns. Electronic systems are primarily French Thomson systems with the TRITON search radar, CASTOR II fire control and VEGA command and control system. A French CSEE PANDA optronic director is also fitted. This design is typical of the late 1970s/early 1980s. (Maritime World Photo Library)

E. The Greek *Antipliarchos Lascos* is typical of a large number of FACs of the French CMN Combattante type that are in service around the world. Again the design dates from the early to mid 1970s and this class of ten units was completed between 1977 and 1981, the later six units being built in Greece. The first four units of this class of 56m boats are armed with four EXOCET anti-ship missiles, the remainder being fitted with six Norwegian PENGUIN anti-ship missiles. Gun armament consists of two Italian 76mm and two twin USA Emersec 30mm guns. In addi-

tion they are fitted with two single 21in torpedo tubes aft which fire a German SST-4 wire-guided active homing torpedo. Electronic outfit comprises the French Thomson VEGA fire control system integrating the TRITON search radar and CASTOR II and POLLUX fire control radars. (Maritime World Photo Library)

F. The Omani FAC *Dhofar* is one of four Province-class 56m FACs built by Vosper Thornycroft in the UK and commissioned between 1982 and 1989. All units are armed with EXOCET anti-ship missiles and Italian OTO Melara 76mm and twin Breda 40mm guns, but carry different electronic outfits. *Dhofar* is fitted with the British SEA ARCHER fire control system, AWS 4 search radar, CUTLASS ESM and SCORPION ECM jammer, and two BARRICADE chaff decoy launchers. The remainder of the class is fitted with the Swedish 307 fire control system and British AWS 6 search radar. Powered by four British Paxman VALENTA diesels, the boats attain a maximum speed of 38 knots. They are interesting in that they are fitted with an electric drive system for slow speed manoeuvring and loitering. They are used extensively to patrol the vital Straits of Hormuz at the entrance to the Persian gulf. (Maritime World Photo Library)

...402 is an updated FPB 38-
...sign built by Lürssen in Ger-
...or the United Arab Emirates.
...ed in mid 1987, the two units
...is class are an enlarged (44m
long) FPB 38 design, powerfully
armed with four EXOCET anti-ship
missiles, an Italian 76mm Super
Rapid gun, a French SADRAL
short-range anti-air missile system
(the first of these systems to be sold
outside France), and British Racal
CUTLASS ESM and CYGNUS
ECM and French CSEE DAGAIE
chaff dispenser electronic warfare
systems. Two German MTU diesels
give a top speed of 34 knots, and the
maximum range is 1,600 nautical
miles at a cruising speed of 16 knots.
(Maritime World Photo Library)

H. Together with the FPB 38 type,
the unit shown here is a Lürssen
Type 62 FAC ordered in mid 1987
for the United Arab Emirates and
completed in 1990, being numbered
P 6201. A second unit is due to be
delivered this year, and a third unit
may be ordered. These units are
designed to operate as leaders to the
other eight FACs owned by the
UAE. They have a maximum speed
of 34–35 knots and a range of 4,000
nautical miles at a cruising speed of
16 knots. Like all other modern
FACs they are powerfully armed,
with anti-ship missiles (eight
EXOCET MM40 missiles), a 76mm
gun, SADRAL point defence missile
system, Dutch GOALKEEPER
CIWS mounted abaft the mast, and
the usual radar and electronic warfare
outfits. A large helicopter landing

platform is sited aft. (Maritime World Photo Library)

I. The Danish Navy has long been an exponent of small fast attack craft. The ten units of the Willemoes class (*Willemoes* is shown here) completed between 1976 and 1978 are typical of the modern FAC, being armed with four US-manufactured HARPOON anti-ship missiles, an Italian 76mm gun, and two 533mm torpedo tubes abreast the bridge. In lieu of the missiles aft and the torpedo tubes the craft can carry twenty mines, or a total of six torpedo tubes and no missiles. The boats are to be updated with a new point defence surface-to-air missile system. They are powered by Rolls-Royce gas turbines and diesel engines. (Maritime World Photo Library)

J. One of the latest designs of fast attack craft is the MGB 62 type built in Germany and Singapore for the Singaporean Navy. Three units are currently operational, and three more are under construction. These 63m craft are armed with eight HARPOON anti-ship missiles, a 76mm OTO Melara Super Rapid gun, two triple torpedo tubes, and will be fitted with a surface-to-air missile system such as the French modular CROTALE, Israeli BARAK or British lightweight SEA WOLF. There is also provision for a PHALANX CIWS. The boats are powered by four MTU diesels giving a maximum speed of 34 knots. The photograph shows *Victory*. (Maritime World Photo Library)

K. The Norwegian *Snarr* is one of six older generation FACs built in 1970–1. These 36.5m boats, powered by two German diesels which give them a speed of 36 knots, are to be modernized with new electronics during the present decade, enabling them to remain in service into the beginning of the next century. They are armed with the Norwegian PENGUIN anti-ship missile (two or four missiles) and four torpedo tubes. Most units carry a Swedish Bofors 40mm gun forward. (Maritime World Photo Library)

L. The largest FACs currently in service are the two FPB 62-001-type Bahraini craft built in Germany. The first unit, *Al Manama* seen here, commissioned in 1988. As the photograph clearly shows, they are distinguished by an extensive helicopter landing platform aft which incorporates an elevator to transport the helicopter to the hangar beneath the landing platform. Armament comprises four EXOCET MM40 anti-ship missiles, a 76mm, twin 40mm and two single 20mm guns. The helicopter carried is the French Dauphin and eight AS-15TT air-to-surface missiles are carried for the helicopter. Electronic systems include Racal CUTLASS and CYGNUS electronic warfare, Swedish SEA GIRAFFE radar, Bofors Electronics 9LV 200 fire control system with 9LV 331 weapon control system. (Maritime World Photo Library)

M. The American hydrofoil *Aquila* is one of a class of six similar missile-armed craft operational with the US Navy. Completed in the early 1980s, it had been planned to build a class of 30 of these craft, some of which would be operated by other NATO navies. Compared to displacement hulled FACs, however, the cost was prohibitive, and only six units were built. The craft are armed with eight HARPOON SSMs, and it had been intended that they would also carry eight reload missiles, but this idea never maerialized. A 76mm gun is mounted forward, and the fire control system is a US derivation of a Dutch Signaal system. The hydrofoils all serve with the US Atlantic Fleet, being based in Florida where they are used on anti-drug patrol duties. (Maritime World Photo Library)

N. The Swedish FAC *Stockholm* (shown here) and her sister ship *Malmo*, although classed as FACs, are really more like small corvettes, so powerfully armed and capable are they with their integrated electronics suite. Armament generally comprises eight Swedish RBS 15 anti-ship missiles, a new Bofors 57mm Mk 2 medium calibre gun, a single 40mm gun aft, two torpedo tubes and four ELMA ASW rocket-launchers. The armament suite is interchangeable, six extra torpedo tubes replacing the missiles and/or mine rails being fitted. Fire control is exercised through a 9LV 300 system with a MARIL weapons control system. (Maritime World Photo Library)

O. The Italian hydrofoil *Nibbio* is one of a class of seven commissioned between 1974 and 1984. Much smaller than the US hydrofoil (23m and 63 tonnes compared to 40.5m and 241 tonnes), they were designed for short duration operations. Powered by Rolls-Royce PROTEUS gas turbines and a waterjet, maximum speeds in the region of 50 knots can be attained in a calm sea. They are considered to be under-powered, however, and there are plans to modernize them with more powerful gas turbines. Armament comprises a 76mm gun forward and two OTOMAT anti-ship missiles. The Japanese Maritime Self Defence Force is to build a class of hydrofoils based on this design. (Maritime World Photo Library)

P. The cramped operations room on board the Italian hydrofoil *Nibbio*, showing the missile control panel (left) and tactical plot (centre). (Maritime World Photo Library)

37. During the 1970s and early 1980s there was a tremendous upsurge in the numbers of missile-armed fast attack craft all over the world, many navies, previously unable to afford powerfully armed large ships, now seeing the possibility of building up their strength using these much cheaper (but still expensive!) small craft armed with anti-ship missiles. To meet the demand shipyards all over the world produced designs for such craft; many of them have never seen the light of day, and some of them were built to specific customer requests and have never been repeated. One such design was that of the Waspada, three of which were built in Singapore by Vosper Singapore for the Royal Brunei Malay Regiment Flotilla. Like so many craft at that time, these boats were armed with the French Aérospatiale EXOCET missile, two of which were mounted aft in their readily recognizable canisters. Forward the craft carried a twin 30mm gun mount. Missile control was exercised through a SEA ARCHER fire control system while the guns were controlled from an optical director. The boats were powered by two MTU diesels which gave them a speed of 32 knots. (Maritime World Photo Library)

38 and 39. Arab states in the Gulf were also quick to note the value of small, fast attack craft. The Sultanate of Oman was among the first to acquire such boats, purchasing a class of seven British Brooke Marine-built 37.5m boats armed with a single 40mm gun forward and aft. The first three completed in 1973 were re-turned to Britain in the mid 1970s to be re-armed with two EXOCET missiles aft and associated SEA ARCHER fire control systems and a twin 40mm gun forward. Unfortunately one of the craft, *Al Bushra*, was lost overboard during a hurricane in the Bay of Biscay from the merchant ship which was carrying her back to Oman. The second batch of four vessels were all completed in 1977 with a 76mm gun forward and a single 20mm gun aft. The first photograph shows *Al Mansur* re-armed with two EXOCET and 40mm gun and the second *Al Fulk* as completed with 76mm and single 20mm guns. (Maritime World Photo Library)

40. During the early 1970s the Greek Navy commissioned four French CMN-built Combattante II-class fast attack craft. These were followed in the early 1980s by ten more Combattante III-type craft, six of which were built in Greece. *Antipliarchos Lascos*, seen here, is a Combattante III-type boat armed with two 76mm guns, two American Emerlec twin 30mm mounts and four EXOCET anti-ship missiles. French surveillance, fire control radars and weapon control systems are fitted and two 21in German torpedo tubes are mounted aft. The Greek-built boats are armed with six Norwegian PENGUIN missiles in lieu of the EXOCETs. (Maritime World Photo Library)

40

41. The Tunisian Combattante III missile craft *La Galite*. These boats follow closely the basic design of the Combattante type with 76mm gun forward, twin 40mm aft, two twin 30mm mounts to the rear of the bridge superstructure and eight EXOCET anti-ship missiles. The latter are of a later design than those illustrated so far. (Maritime World Photo Library)

42. Iran also purchased ten Combattante II-type craft during the late 1970s–early 1980s. Again the basic design remained the same, but armament differed. The 76mm gun was retained, but an older single 40mm was mounted aft and no 30mm were fitted. Instead of the EXOCET missiles, four American HARPOON anti-ship missiles were fitted. One of this class was sunk by Iraq in 1980 and another by US forces in 1988. As Iran can no longer obtain spares for the HARPOON missiles, it is possible that they may be replaced with Chinese anti-ship missiles, China having become a regular supplier of military equipment to Iran following the fall of the Shah. (Maritime World Photo Library)

43. During the mid 1960s the Royal Swedish Navy commissioned six fast attack craft of the Spica I-class (*Spica* herself is seen here). The boats were armed with a 57mm gun forward of the bridge and six 21in torpedo tubes, one set of two abreast the gun and the remaining four abreast the bridge to port and starboard. The fire control system was the Dutch M22 system, mounted in a large radome on top of the bridge. Power was provided by three British PROTEUS gas turbines which gave a speed of 40 knots. (Maritime World Photo Library)

44

44 and 45. The Spica I class was followed by twelve boats of the Spica II class commissioned from 1973 to 1976. The design used the same hull as the previous class with the same propulsion and armament, but had a different fire control system. The second photograph shows a boat of the Spica II class as originally completed. During the early 1980s the class was extensively modernized and became known as the Norrkoping class. The hulls and machinery were completely refurbished and armament and all electronics systems completely renewed. New 57mm guns were fitted and in an innovative move FACs were, for the first time, equipped with hull-mounted sonar – in this case an active, high-frequency system. A new air/surface search radar, the Swedish SEA GIRAFFE G-band, was fitted and the latest fire control system, the Swedish 9LV 200 J-band system. In addition the boats were equipped to mount eight RBS 15 anti-ship missile-launchers right aft. A number of boats are also fitted with the ELMA 9-tube anti-submarine mortar launcher. An ESM electronic warfare radar intercept system, the Saab EWS 905, is also fitted. The photographs shows *Pitea* as modernized. (Maritime World Photo Library)

46. The anti-ship missile deployed by the Swedish Norrkoping class is the RBS 15, which has a range of 70 kilometres. The missile is guided to its target using active radar homing. The photograph shows an RBS 15 missile leaving the launch tube of the FAC *Pitea*. (Maritime World Photo Library)

47. During the late 1970s–early 1980s Sweden commissioned a smaller class of FAC, the sixteen boats of the Hugin class. Of only 150 tons full load (compared to the 230 tons full load displacement of the Norrkoping class), these boats could only mount a smaller anti-ship missile system. The system chosen was the Norwegian PENGUIN, six of which are carried. The boats are also armed with the ELMA anti-submarine mortar, and a 57mm gun. Aft two mine rails extend over the stern enabling 24 mines to be carried in lieu of the missile-launchers. This is a feature common to all Swedish FACs in that missile/mine/torpedo fits are completely interchangeable, depending on the anticipated threat and mission requirement. These boats are also fitted with a sonar, the Norwegian Simrad SQ 3D/SF hull-mounted, active, high-frequency system. The craft are powered by two MTU diesel engines uprated and refitted after removal from an earlier class of patrol boat deleted from the Swedish Navy. The Hugin class is to be modernized during the second half of this decade, with new sonar, possibly a VDS system, improved combat information system, ASW weapons and new machinery outfit. (Maritime World Photo Library)

48. The Swedish Hugin-class FAC *Mjolner*, showing four PENGUIN missile-launchers aft and the mine/depth-charge rails with four depth-charges. (L. van Ginderen, via Maritime World Photo Library)

49. The popularity of the FAC rapidly spread to many smaller navies around the world throughout the 1970s and early 1980s. Malaysia was one of the first of the Far Eastern navies to see the potential of the FAC as a means of rapidly expanding her naval capability. The four Perdana-class missile-armed boats, built by CMN in France to the Combattante II design, were commissioned in the early 1970s. Armament comprised two Aérospatiale EXOCET anti-ship missile-launchers aft and a Swedish Bofors 57mm gun forward, fire control for the guns being exercised through a French Thomson-CSF VEGA system. Missile control was provided by a Thomsen-CSF POLLUX I/J-band radar with a Thomson-CSF TRITON radar for air/surface search. The illustration shows *Serang*. (NAVPIC via Maritime World Photo Library)

50. The six Jerong-class boats built in the Far East to a German Lürssen Type 45 design were the next class to be acquired by Malaysia. These were gun-armed craft and, like the previous class, carried a Swedish Bofors 57mm forward and a Bofors 40mm aft, but no missiles. They were powered by three German Maybach/Mercedes Benz diesel engines which gives them a speed of 32 knots. A Dutch WM 28 fire control system provides weapon control, with a British Decca 626 radar providing surface search capabilities. The photograph shows *Todak* in May 1990. (G. Toremans via Maritime World Photo Library)

51. In the late 1970s Malaysia ordered four FACs from Sweden to a modified Spica design. These were commissioned in 1979. The boats are armed with four EXOCET anti-ship missiles, a Bofors 57mm gun forward and a 40mm aft and, like the Swedish boats, carry a hull-mounted Norwegian sonar. If required the boats can be fitted with torpedo tubes. (Maritime World Photo Library)

52. During the late 1970s, when so many FACs were being seen all over the world, Yugoslavia commissioned a class of six indigenously designed FACs. Like the Malaysian boats, the design was based on the Swedish *Spica*, but was drawn up by the Naval Shipping Institute in Yugoslavia. Propulsion is provided by a mix of two Rolls-Royce PROTEUS gas turbines and two MTU diesels. Armament comprises two Soviet-designed STYX anti-ship missiles mounted aft and a Bofors 57mm gun forward, with Swedish electronics. (Maritime World Photo Library)

53. In the late 1960s Israel, despite political problems, managed to acquire 10 FACs known as the Saar type. These craft were built to a German Lürssen design by CMN in France, and in spite of an arms embargo, managed to reach Israel. The first batch of six craft carry various armament configurations including a single 40mm and GABRIEL anti-ship missiles, to three 40mm and four torpedo tubes and a sonar. Although originally referred to as Saar 1-type craft, this batch is now referred to as Saar 2. The second batch of four craft (known as Saar 3) are fitted for a mix of HARPOON long-range and shorter-range Israeli-designed and manufactured GABRIEL anti-ship missiles as well as a 76mm gun forward, but no sonar is fitted. The photograph shows a Saar 3-type vessel armed with three GABRIEL and two HARPOON missile-launchers. (Maritime World Photo Library)

54. Following acquisition of the Saar 2 and 3, Israel developed the design further and built eight Reshef-class (Saar 4) FACs at the Haifa shipyard which were commissioned from 1973 to 1980. These are much larger than the previous boats (58m long compared to 45m, and 450 tons full load compared to 250 tons full load) and carry a much more powerful armament comprising one or two 76mm guns, two Oerlikon 20mm and a full range of electronic warfare systems including threat warners, jammers and decoys. Missile armament comprises two/four HARPOON and four/six GABRIEL anti-ship missiles. In recent years some boats have been fitted with the American PHALANX close-in weapon system. Some boats in the class will have the PHALANX replaced by the Israeli-developed vertical-launch BARAK anti-air missile system. A remarkable feature of these Saar designs is their extraordinary endurance. The first boats made the journey from France to Israel unaided. The Reshef class has an endurance of 4,000 nautical miles at 17.5 knots and exhibits very high seakeeping qualities, as witness a passage made by some of the class from Israel to the Red Sea via the Straits of Gibraltar and the Cape of Good Hope, being refuelled at sea on the way. It was during this voyage that the craft were demonstrated to the South African Defence Forces, who themselves subsequently

ordered three from the Haifa Shipyard. The photograph shows a Reshef-class boat armed with two 76mm and four GABRIEL and a quadruple HARPOON missile-launchers. Some of this class have been transferred to the Chilean Navy in recent years. (Maritime World Photo Library)

55. The Israeli GABRIEL anti-ship missile system, developed as a counter to the Soviet-built STYX system then entering service in large numbers with Arab navies, first entered service in 1972, being used in action during the 1973 Yom Kippur War. Its success during this war led to large numbers of the weapon being sold to other navies including Taiwan, Kenya, Ecuador, Singapore, Thailand and South Africa. The South African SKERPIOEN missile is derived from the

GABRIEL built under licence, while the Taiwanese HSIUNG FENG I is an unlicensed copy. Four versions of the GABRIEL have been developed, the Mk III (seen here being launched from an Israeli FAC) having a range of 60 kilometres. (Maritime World Photo Library)

56. During the early 1980s Israel commissioned four 61.7m, 488 tons full load Saar 4.5 FACs. The acquisition of the American long-range HARPOON anti-ship missile required some form of mid-course guidance and to provide the data for this it was decided to equip the Aliya with an on-board helicopter, which led to the fitting of a large hangar aft and a landing platform. Eventually only the first two units were fitted with the hangar, a 76mm gun and four GABRIEL missile-launchers replacing the hangar structure in the next two. Armament in the first two units comprises four HARPOON missile-launchers sited between the hangar and the bridge superstructure, and four GABRIEL missile-launchers forward (the later two vessels mount eight HARPOON and eight GABRIEL) and in the later boats a 76mm aft and a PHALANX CIWS forward. The photograph is of *Aliya*. (Maritime World Photo Library)

57. At the end of the 1970s Israel drew up plans to acquire a fleet of twelve missile-armed hydrofoils, the design of which was based on the American Grumman Company's *Flagstaff*. The first boat was ordered from Grumman and was launched in May 1981, it being intended that the remainder be ordered from an Israeli shipyard. To date only three of the class have been built, the last, *Snapirit* (seen here) being completed in June 1985. No more of the class have been ordered and it would seem that proposals to build a class of twelve have been dropped. Armament comprises four HARPOON and two GABRIEL missile-launchers, and a twin 30mm gun mounting forward of the bridge. The boats are powered by two American gas turbines which give them a speed of 48 knots. Fire control systems and EW aerials are all carried in the distinctive radome mounted above the bridge. (Maritime World Photo Library)

58 and 59. Following the presentation of the Saar boats to South Africa, a contract was signed for three boats of a similar design to be built in Israel and six in South Africa. All were completed from 1977 to 1986. Armament consists of six South African-built SKERPIOEN missiles, the Israeli GABRIEL built under licence, two 76mm guns and two 20mm. French surveillance radar and Italian fire control systems comprise the electronics. The photographs show a South African Minister-class FAC on patrol, and one just having fired a SKERPIOEN anti-ship missile. (Maritime World Photo Library)

60. During the late 1970s Egypt ordered a class of six 52m Ramadan-class FACs from Vosper Thornycroft in the UK. Completed in 1981–82 this was a custom-built design, the requirement being for a large craft of some 300 tons full load, carrying a heavy armament of four OTOMAT anti-ship missiles, a 76mm and twin 40mm guns. Extensive electronic systems are fitted which include a Ferranti CAAIS combat information suite, a Marconi SAPPHIRE fire control system with two ST 802 combined radar/TV trackers and two optical directors, and a Marconi S 810 combined air/surface search radar housed in a distinctive radome just behind the bridge. Electronic warfare systems comprise a Racal CUTLASS ESM radar intercept sensor and CYGNUS ECM jammer and chaff/IR decoy launchers. The boats are powered by four MTU diesels which give a speed of 40 knots. The photograph shows *Khyber* leaving Portsmouth bound for Alexandria, minus the OTOMAT missile-launchers. The pennant numbers were changed shortly after commissioning, 562 becoming 672. (Maritime World Photo Library)

60

61. While the Ramadan class was under construction, Vosper Thornycroft were also modernizing six Egyptian-built, Russian October-class FACs. The boats were almost completely rebuilt, being re-engined with Italian CRM diesels, two OTOMAT missile-launchers, twin 30mm gun mounts, Marconi radar and fire control systems compatible with the Ramadan class and a radar threat warning system. The craft are now obsolete and will probably be scrapped shortly. (Maritime World Photo Library)

62. By the mid 1980s FAC construction had largely died down, with only a few new designs being built, and these in small numbers of two/three per type. Instead, construction tended towards somewhat larger boats which were really small corvettes of between 600–1,000 tonnes. Only the Soviet Union continued to build FACs in large numbers. One of their designs was the Pauk class, construction of which began in 1977 and of which a total of 34 have been completed so far with construction continuing. These 57.8m craft are armed with a 76mm gun forward, a 6-barrelled 30mm on the after superstructure, a quadruple GRAIL SA-N-5 missile-launcher on a disappearing mount in front of the bridge and four 16in torpedo tubes abreast the superstructure. Also abreast the superstructure are two 5-barrelled RBU-1200 ASW mortars. Extensive electronics are fitted, including a variable-depth sonar mounted on the transom aft in a distinctive housing. (Maritime World Photo Library)

63. Apart from the Soviet Union, the only other navy to embark on a programme of FAC construction of any size was Germany, with the Type 143A – the Gepard class. These 57.6m craft, powered by four MTU diesels with a speed of 40 knots, are constructed with wooden hulls carried on aluminium framing. The layout follows the standard pattern of 76mm gun forward and four EXOCET anti-ship missiles aft. In due course it is planned that the boats will carry the RAM point defence missile system behind the EXOCETs. The craft are fitted with extensive electronic warfare systems and the latest AGIS combat information system to co-ordinate the sensors and weapons. A total of ten boats were built from 1982 to 1984. The photograph of *Hermelin* shows clearly mine-laying rails extending aft, and the space available for the RAM system. (B. Prezelin via Maritime World Photo Library)

64. During the late 1970s Finland designed a new class of FAC – the Helsinki class – four of which were completed from 1981 to 1986. These 300-ton full load, 45m craft carry four/eight Swedish Saab RBS 15 anti-ship missiles, a Bofors 57mm gun, and two twin Soviet 30mm guns. Swedish radar and fire control systems are carried, and a Norwegian Simrad sonar is fitted. Although the standard armament is quoted, this can be varied to suit the operational role. (Maritime World Photo Library)

65

66

65, 66 and 67. During the 1980s a number of Arab Gulf countries embarked on the acquisition of small numbers of FACs. From 1982 to 1989 Oman acquired four Province-class FACs, with slightly differing armament and electronics. The first to be completed, *Dhofar* (Photograph No. 65), was commissioned in 1982 and armed with six MM40 EXOCET missiles and a Plessey AWS 4 radar. Extensive electronic warfare equipment was also fitted, and the craft are powered by four Paxman diesels. Later units in the class carry eight EXOCET and different electronic systems. The second unit, *Al Sharqiyah* (Photograph No. 66) is seen on sea trials during 1983. The last unit to be completed, *Mussandam* (Photograph No. 67), is fitted with the Plessey AWS 6 radar and eight EXOCET missiles. All units carry a 76mm gun. (Maritime World Photo Library)

67

68. Kuwait, another Arab Gulf state, also acquired FACs during the 1980s, six German Lürssen-built TNC 45 (45m) craft being ordered in 1980. These are armed with four EXOCET missiles, a 76mm and twin 40mm guns, Swedish fire control and radar systems and extensive electronic warfare equipment. They entered service in 1983/4. Some of this class were sunk during the war with Iraq early in 1991. The photograph is of *Al Boom*. (Maritime World Photo Library)

69. In 1980 Kuwait also ordered two much larger FACs from Lürssen which were designed to operate as flotilla leaders for the TNC 45s. These 58m, 410-ton craft carry an armament of four EXOCET missiles, a 76mm and twin 40mm guns and have a minelaying capability. Extensive electronics are fitted, including full surveillance radar and fire control and a comprehensive electronic warfare suite. The photograph is of *Sabhan*. (L. van Ginderen via Maritime World Photo Library)

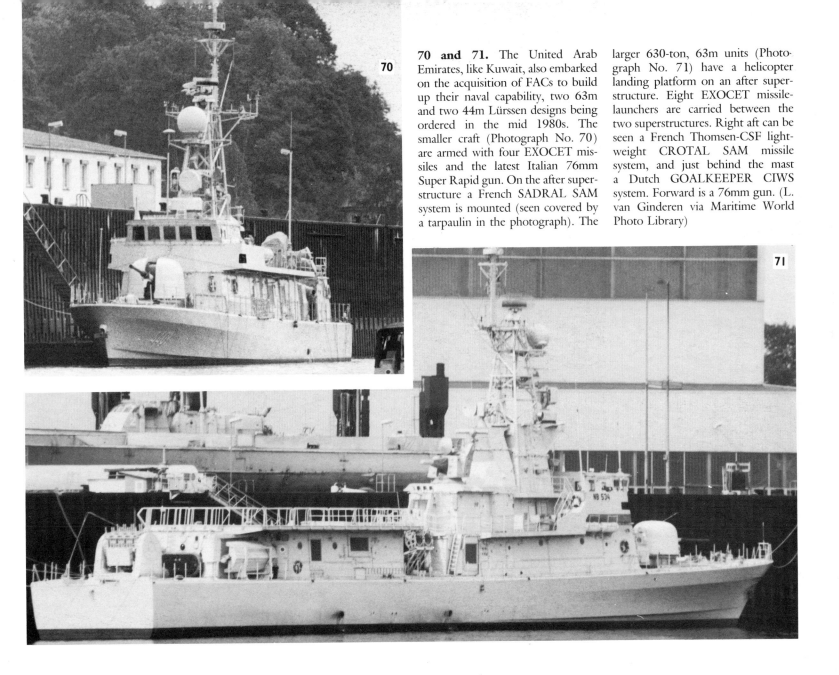

70 and 71. The United Arab Emirates, like Kuwait, also embarked on the acquisition of FACs to build up their naval capability, two 63m and two 44m Lürssen designs being ordered in the mid 1980s. The smaller craft (Photograph No. 70) are armed with four EXOCET missiles and the latest Italian 76mm Super Rapid gun. On the after superstructure a French SADRAL SAM system is mounted (seen covered by a tarpaulin in the photograph). The larger 630-ton, 63m units (Photograph No. 71) have a helicopter landing platform on an after superstructure. Eight EXOCET missile-launchers are carried between the two superstructures. Right aft can be seen a French Thomsen-CSF lightweight CROTAL SAM missile system, and just behind the mast a Dutch GOALKEEPER CIWS system. Forward is a 76mm gun. (L. van Ginderen via Maritime World Photo Library)

72. Like the UAE, Bahrain also acquired large FACs with a helicopter handling capability. Similar in concept to the Israeli *Aliya*, the two Lürssen FPB 62-type craft incorporate a hangar with an integral lift to take the helicopter below. A French Dauphin helicopter is embarked for which AS 15TT anti-ship missiles are carried. Two units were commissioned in 1987/8 and armament consists of two EXOCET missile-launchers sited between the bridge superstructure and the hangar, a 76mm gun forward and twin 40mm aft, and full electronic outfit comprising surveillance and fire control radars, and EW systems. (L. van Ginderen via Maritime World Photo Library)

73. In 1987 Kenya commissioned two 56m FACs similar in design to the Omani Province class. Built by Vosper Thornycroft, they are armed with four OTOMAT missiles, 76mm gun forward and twin 30mm gun on the after superstructure, two single 20mm on the bridge, a Ferranti CAAIS combat information system and comprehensive electronic equipment. (Maritime World Photo Library)

74. Among the latest FACs to be commissioned are the five Type PB 57 craft for the Indonesian Navy. The first of these was built by Lürssen in Germany and outfitted in Indonesia. The remaining craft, including a further three projected units, are being built in Indonesia. Of 423 tons full load and 58 metres long, these boats are armed with the latest Bofors 57mm Mk 2 gun and a Bofors 40mm aft. Two 21in torpedo tubes are mounted in the stern. Electronics systems include a LIOD optronics director on the first two (Selenia NA 18 on the remainder) mounted on top of the bridge, a Dutch WM 22 fire control radar mounted in a large radome on the small mast, French electronic warfare outfit and DAGAIE chaff/IR decoy launcher and Racal Decca surface search radar. The third and fourth units are probably outfitted for an ASW role carrying a Dutch PHS 32 sonar. Power is provided by two MTU diesels which give a maximum speed of 27 knots. The photograph shows *Singa*, the second unit to be commissioned (in 1988). The fifth unit was commissioned at the beginning of this year. (G. Toremans via Maritime World Photo Library)

75. Finally Singapore is building a squadron of six Victory-class FACs based on the German Lürssen MGB 62 design, variants of which are in service in Bahrain and the UAE (see above). These feature a very low silhouette to minimize radar signature and have a very distinctive high mast to obtain satisfactory radar horizon ranges. The entire hull and superstructure is specifically designed to reduce the overall radar signature to a minimum. The boats displace 500 tons full load on a length of 62 metres. Propulsion consists of four MTU diesels which give a speed of 35 knots. Armament consists of eight HARPOON missiles, 76mm gun and six 324mm torpedo tubes in two triple mounts mounted aft. A full electronic warfare outfit is carried and standard electronics include a Dutch ZW 06 surveillance radar and variable-depth sonar. It is understood that the boats are equipped with a Dutch combat information system. The photograph shows the first of class, *Victory*, which was commissioned in 1990. (G. Toremans via Maritime World Photo Library)

75

Class-Name	Osa II	Combattante III	Pauk	Shershen	Turya	Stenka
Country of Origin	USSR	France	USSR	USSR	USSR	USSR
Displacement (tonnes):						
standard	165	345	N/A	145	190	170
full load	210	395	440	170	250	210
Dimensions (metres):						
length (oa)	39.00	56.00	57.80	34.7	39.6	39
beam	7.80	8.20	9.40	6.7	12.5	7.8
draught	1.80	2.20	2.30	1.5	1.8	1.8
Armament:						
missiles	four STYX SS-N-2	eight EXOCET	SA-N-5 GRAIL	n/f	n/f	n/f
guns	two twin 30mm	one 76mm	one 76mm	two twin 30mm	one twin 57mm	two twin 30mm
		one twin 40mm	one 30mm	one twin 25mm		
		two 30mm				
Torpedoes	n/f	n/f	four 406mm	four 533mm	four 533mm	four 406mm
Propulsion:						
system	Diesel	Diesel	Diesel	Diesel	Diesel	Diesel
No. & power (bhp)	3×15,000	4×19,300	4×16,000	3×12,000	3×15,000	3×12,000
Speed (knots):	40	38.5	32	45	40	36

Electronics:	Osa II	Combattante III	Pauk	Shershen	Turya	Stenka
Radar	SQUARE TIE	N/A	PEEL CONE SPIN TROUGH	POT HEAD	POT DRUM	POT DRUM
fire control	DRUM TILT	NAJA (1)	BASS TILT	DRUM TILT	MUFF COB	DRUM TILT
Sonar	n/f	n/f	VDS	n/f	VDS	VDS
EW	n/f	DAGAIE (2)	ESM + Chaff	N/A	N/A	N/A
Endurance:						
(nautical miles/knots)	800/30	700/33	N/A	850/30	600/35	800/24
Complement	30	42	32	23	30	30

Class-Name	Victory	Helsinki	Stockholm	FPB 45	FPB 57	Saar 4
Country of Origin	Singapore	Finland	Sweden	Germany	Germany	Israel
Displacement (tonnes):						
standard	N/A	280	310	–	–	N/A
full load	550	300	335	259	410	488
Dimensions (metres):						
length (oa)	62	45	50	44.9	58.1	61.7
beam	8.5	8.9	6.8	7	7.6	7.6
draught	2.5	3	1.9	2.5	2.7	2.5
Armament:						
missiles	eight HARPOON	four RBS 15	eight RBS 15	two EXOCET	four EXOCET	eight HARPOON eight GABRIEL
guns	one 76mm	one 57mm two twin 23mm	one 57mm one 40mm	one 76mm	one 76mm	one 76mm two 20mm PHALANX CIWS
Torpedoes	six 324mm	n/f	four 400mm	n/f	n/f	n/f
Propulsion:						
system	Diesel	Diesel	Diesel + GT	Diesel	Diesel	Diesel
No. & power (bhp)	4×18,740	3×11,000	1×6,000shp (GT) 2×4,200	4×15,400	4×18,000	4×14,000
Speed (knots):	35	30	32 (GT)	40	36	31
Electronics:						
Radar	ZW 06	9GA 208	SEA GIRAFFE	LV200	Marconi S 810	NEPTUNE
fire control	9LV 200 Mk3	EOS 400	9LV 200 Mk 3	PANDA (1)	9 LV 200	ORION RTN 10X
Sonar	EDO 780 VDS	SS 304	SS 304	n/f	n/f	n/f
EW	DAGAIE (2) + EW	ESM + MATILDA	EWS 905 + PHILAX	RDL 2 + DAGAIE	ESM + DAGAIE	MN 53 ESM + Chaff
Endurance:						
(nautical miles/knots)	4,000/18	N/A	N/A	1,600/16	1,300/30	4,000/17
Complement	46	30	40	36	40	45

Notes: The specifications given above are general, and units operational in different navies show considerable variations in equipment. n/f not fitted. N/A no details available (1) Optronic system (2) Chaff/IR decoy launcher.

FPB 62 type as supplied to Bahrain.

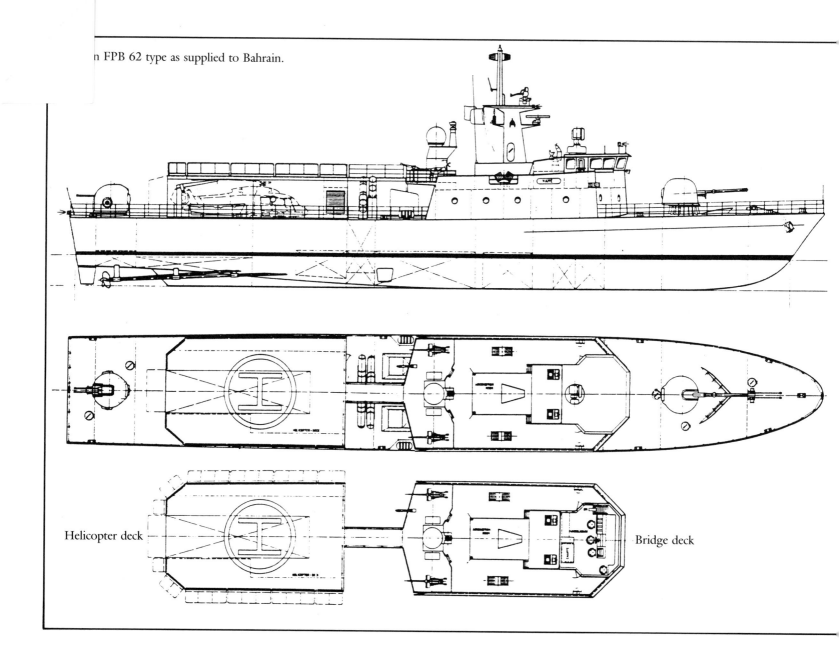

Helicopter deck

Bridge deck

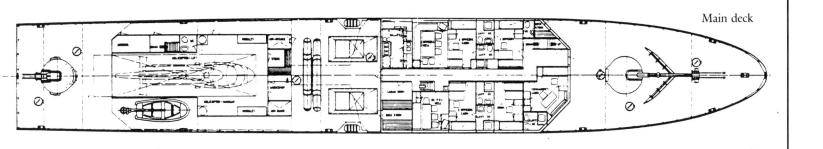

Main deck

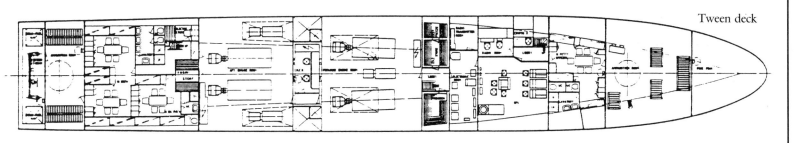

Tween deck

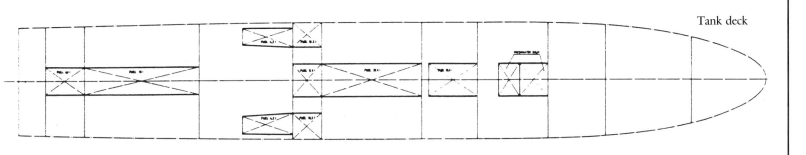

Tank deck

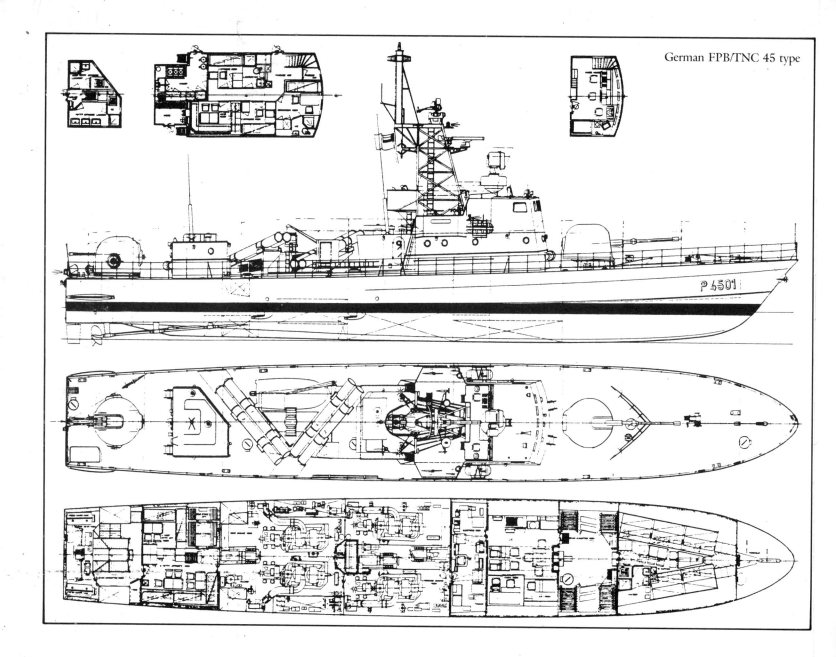

German FPB/TNC 45 type

P 4501